Space

Surviving in Zero-G

by Donna Latham

Consultant: Michelle Nichols, Master Educator
Adler Planetarium & Astronomy Museum
Chicago, Illinois

BEARPORT
PUBLISHING COMPANY, INC.

New York, New York

CREDITS
Cover, NASA (National Aeronautics and Space Administration); Title page, NASA (National Aeronautics and Space Administration); 4(L&R), NASA (National Aeronautics and Space Administration); 5, NASA (National Aeronautics and Space Administration); 6, NASA (National Aeronautics and Space Administration); 7, GoodShoot/SuperStock; 8, Steve Stankiewitz; 9, Science Photo Library/Photo Researcher, Inc.; 10, NASA (National Aeronautics and Space Administration); 11, NASA (National Aeronautics and Space Administration); 12, NASA (National Aeronautics and Space Administration); 13, NASA/Roger Ressmeyer/Corbis; 14, NASA (National Aeronautics and Space Administration); 15, NASA (National Aeronautics and Space Administration); 16, NASA (National Aeronautics and Space Administration); 17, NASA (National Aeronautics and Space Administration); 18, NASA (National Aeronautics and Space Administration); 19, NASA (National Aeronautics and Space Administration); 20, NASA (National Aeronautics and Space Administration); 21, NASA (National Aeronautics and Space Administration); 22, Roger Ressmeyer/Corbis; 23, NASA (National Aeronautics and Space Administration); 24(L&R), NASA (National Aeronautics and Space Administration); 25, NASA (National Aeronautics and Space Administration); 26, NASA (National Aeronautics and Space Administration); 27, NASA (National Aeronautics and Space Administration); 29, NASA (National Aeronautics and Space Administration).

EDITORIAL DEVELOPMENT by Judy Nayer
DESIGN & PRODUCTION by Paula Jo Smith

Special thanks to Susan Erskin, Media Resource Center, Tessada & Associates, NASA/Johnson Space Center

Library of Congress Cataloging-in-Publication Data

Latham, Donna.
  Space : surviving in zero-G / by Donna Latham.
    p. cm.—(X-treme places)
  Includes bibliographical references and index.
  ISBN 1-59716-090-3 (library binding)—ISBN 1-59716-127-6 (pbk.)
1. Extravehicular activity (Manned space flight)—Juvenile literature. 2. Space flights—Juvenile literature.
3. Godwin, Linda M. (Linda Maxine), 1952—Juvenile literature. 4. Tani, Daniel M., 1961—Juvenile literature.
5. Astronautics—United States—Juvenile literature. I. Title. II. Series.

TL1096.L38 2006
629.45'84—dc22
                         2005006575

For more information, write to Bearport Publishing Company, Inc., 101 Fifth Avenue, Suite 6R, New York, New York 10003. Printed in the United States of America.

1 2 3 4 5 6 7 8 9 10

Contents

A Walk in Space

It was December 10, 2001. Astronauts Linda Godwin and Dan Tani were ready. Months of training on the ground had led to this moment. It was time to take a walk in space!

Dr. Linda M. Godwin

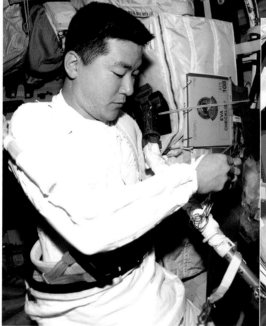
Daniel M. Tani

Linda and Dan were suited up in $12 million space suits. They were going to make repairs on the **International Space Station** (ISS).

Wearing bulky space suits, Linda and Dan left the main cabin of the **space shuttle** *Endeavour*. They entered the sealed **airlock** and opened a tap. Air burst out with a whoosh. Soon, the air was gone. They could safely leave the shuttle.

Linda and Dan floated into the darkness. They faced a job full of risks. They had to survive in one of the most extreme places in the universe—space.

More than 150 miles (241 km) above Earth, the ISS moves around the planet at 17,500 miles per hour (28,164 kph).

What Is Space?

   As astronauts, Linda and Dan leave Earth to live and work in space. Space is also called *outer space*. It is everything outside Earth's atmosphere—the layer of air around our planet. Most scientists agree that space begins about 60 miles (97 km) above Earth.

The moon is Earth's closest neighbor in space. Astronauts first landed on the moon in 1969.

Earth is huge. It is home to six billion people. That number increases every day. At the **equator**, Earth is almost 25,000 miles (40,234 km) around. Yet, in the **vastness** of space, Earth is just a tiny speck.

Space is enormous. All the planets, their moons, and billions and billions of stars travel through space. The distance between objects in space is very large.

Because distances in space are so huge, they are measured in light years. A light year is the distance light travels in one year— 5.9 trillion miles (9.5 trillion km).

How big is space? No one knows for sure. Scientists aren't even certain whether it ends or goes on forever.

Our Solar System

Everything in space moves—usually around something else. Linda and Dan's spaceship moved around Earth at a speed of about five miles per second (8 kps).

People on Earth are also moving through space. Our planet **orbits**, or circles around, the sun, which is a giant star. The sun and all the planets that orbit it form our **solar system**.

OUR SOLAR SYSTEM

In our solar system nine planets—including Earth—circle, or orbit, the sun.

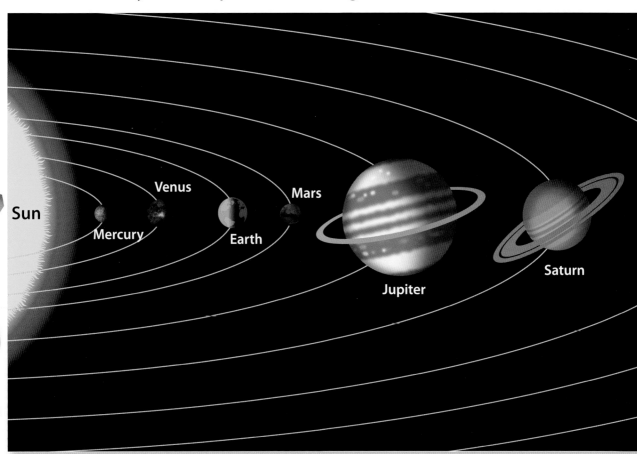

Sun

Mercury

Venus

Earth

Mars

Jupiter

Saturn

Comets, asteroids, and meteoroids are also moving through space. Comets have glowing tails and are made mostly of ice and dust. Asteroids are chunks of rock and metal—some are small, but some are as large as planets. Meteoroids are rocky chunks that are smaller than comets and asteroids.

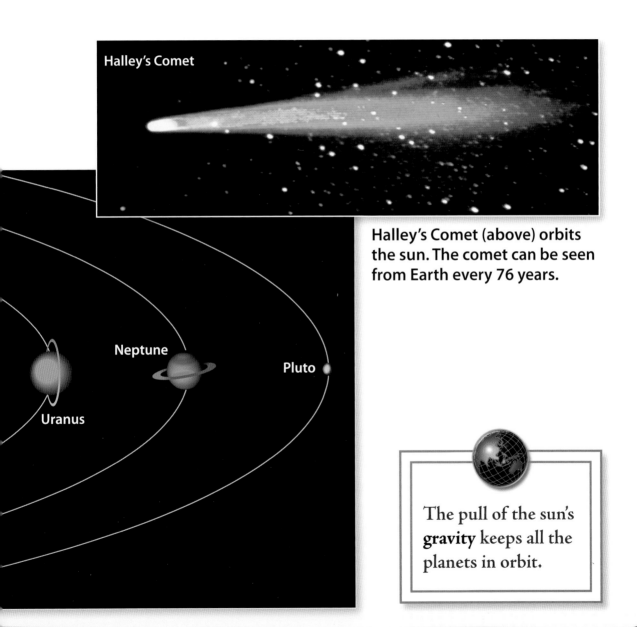

Halley's Comet

Halley's Comet (above) orbits the sun. The comet can be seen from Earth every 76 years.

Neptune

Pluto

Uranus

The pull of the sun's **gravity** keeps all the planets in orbit.

People and Space

It's difficult for living things to survive in space. In fact, people can only live there when they bring with them everything they need to stay alive!

Astronauts enter and leave the ISS through this airlock.

The first crew moved into the ISS in 2000. Where is the ISS right now? Check science.nasa.gov/temp/StationLoc.html to find out!

So far, Earth is the only place where we know life exists. Yet scientists at **NASA** keep searching. Since space is so vast, many people think life must exist other places in the universe, too.

Today, 16 countries are united in exploring space. Together, they are building the ISS, where explorers can safely live and work.

Two astronauts work on the ISS in 1998.

Suited Up for Survival

The human body is not built to survive in space. There is no air to breathe. There is little gravity. Astronauts call it zero gravity, or zero-G.

In zero-G, people are **weightless**. Muscles and bones get weaker because they don't have to work hard. Spines get longer, since spine bones don't stay pressed together. So astronauts often have backaches.

In space, astronauts exercise two hours a day. Here, Shannon Lucid (LOO-sid) runs on a treadmill.

Zero-G causes blood to collect in the head and upper body. Astronauts appear puffy-cheeked and scrawny-legged.

Linda and Dan knew of these dangers. They counted on their space suits to protect them.

Space Survival Equipment

Space suits have everything astronauts need to stay alive in space.

Visors—one gold, to block the sun's harmful rays; one clear, for work in darkness

Earphones and Microphone *(under the helmet)*—**for talking to shuttle crew and mission control on Earth**

Portable Life Support System—with electrical power and oxygen

Helmet—with a TV camera and lights

Gloves—with rubber fingertips to hold tools

Space Suit—made of 12 layers to protect against extreme cold and heat

Drink Bag *(not pictured)*—with a tube leading into the helmet to supply water

Boots—to keep astronauts from drifting away

Kathy Sullivan, the first American woman to walk in space, calls the space suit "a body-shaped spaceship."

Training

Linda and Dan trained to learn how to survive in space. To prepare for extreme temperatures, they went to the frozen Canadian wilderness for winter survival training. The astronauts spent a week together building shelters and finding food and water.

To train for working in weightlessness, Linda and Dan plunged into the Neutral Buoyancy Lab (NBL). This pool is 40 feet (12 m) deep and 202 feet (62 m) long. The NBL holds a whopping 6.2 million gallons (23.5 million l) of water.

Astronauts practice winter survival skills.

Linda and Dan wore 250-pound (113-kg) space suits underwater. In the pool, they practiced using tools for their space walk.

The NBL is large enough to hold the entire space shuttle. In it, astronauts get used to weightlessness—and to wearing their space suits.

Wearing space suits underwater gives astronauts the same feeling they will have when they float in space. Training sessions in the NBL lasted seven hours.

A Ride on the Robot Arm

As they floated outside *Endeavour*, Linda and Dan were **tethered** to the shuttle's **robot arm**. The tethers were lifelines that kept the astronauts from drifting off into space. If Linda and Dan got lost from their ship, they would die. In hours, their oxygen would run out and they would suffocate.

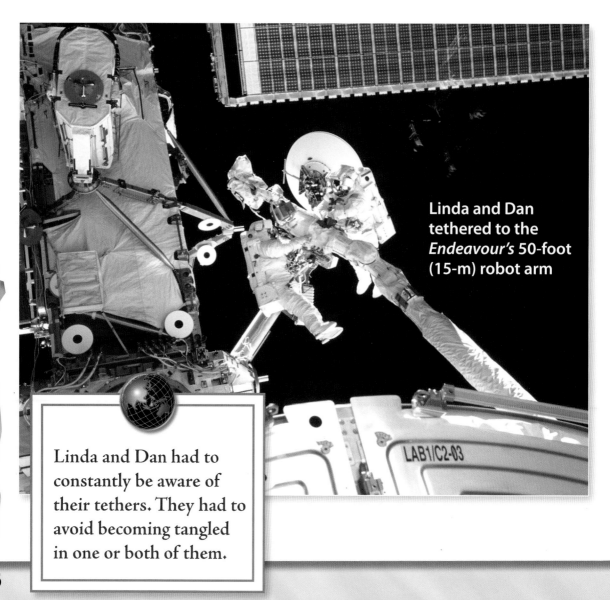

Linda and Dan tethered to the *Endeavour's* 50-foot (15-m) robot arm

Linda and Dan had to constantly be aware of their tethers. They had to avoid becoming tangled in one or both of them.

Inside *Endeavour*, pilot Mark Kelly worked the robot arm. Linda and Dan hitched a ride halfway up the space station's huge power tower. Below, the Pacific Ocean was in sight. The spacewalkers had the best view in the universe.

"A beautiful Earth down there," Linda called.

"The view is impossible to describe," Dan agreed.

In the 1980s, astronaut Bruce McCandless tested this jet backpack.

Wrapped in Blankets

Linda and Dan had important repair work to do. The motors that turned the station's **solar wings** had been shutting down. Extreme temperatures were to blame. Linda and Dan needed to wrap **thermal** blankets around the motors to keep them warm.

The solar wings spread 240 feet (73 m) across, about the length of a football field. They are covered with 32,800 solar cells. The cells change sunlight into electricity.

Solar wings use the sun's energy to provide power to the space station.

The astronauts jumped onto the power tower. They climbed 50 feet (15 m) in their stiff suits, while still tethered to the robot arm.

Then, together, Linda and Dan unfolded a blanket. They struggled to attach it to the motor. Their bulky gloves slowed them down. Soon, however, they had fastened all but one strap to hold the blanket in place.

"You guys did a great job," said mission commander Dom Gorie.

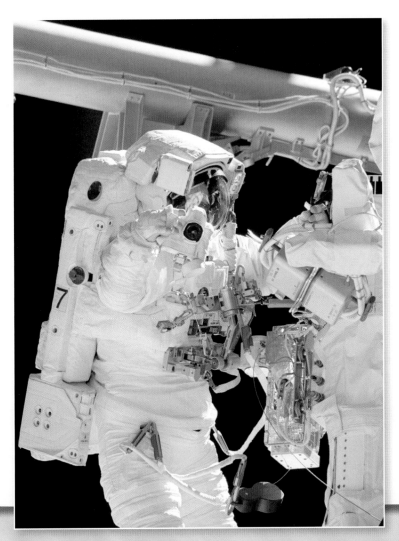

During the repairs, Dan took pictures.

Hot and Cold

Linda and Dan zipped through space at 17,500 miles per hour (28,164 kph). They saw a sunrise or sunset every 45 minutes. In the blink of an eye, light became dark. The sight was amazing. Still, the constant changes brought extreme temperatures.

In sunlight, Linda holds the robot arm.

Even working side-by-side, Linda and Dan faced wildly different temperatures. Since they were constantly moving, one astronaut might be in the sun's light while the other worked in darkness.

In sunlight, the temperature climbed to 250°F (121°C). In the Earth's shadow, it plunged to -140°F (-96°C). Linda and Dan experienced roasting heat and bitter cold. Yet, inside their suits, their bodies stayed at safe temperatures.

Little bits of dust drifted through space. Though tiny, they could be deadly. Layers of material that made up the astronaut's suit kept space junk from ripping through.

Linda and Dan work near the end of *Endeavour's* robot arm.

Getting a Grip

The "hand work" on a space walk is especially difficult. The gloves are **pressurized** with air making it hard to grip tools. Spacewalkers must squeeze their gloves nonstop. Their hands and arms grow tired.

Astronauts say that the toughest part of a space walk is using gloves to grab tools and equipment. The effort is like squeezing a rubber ball for hours.

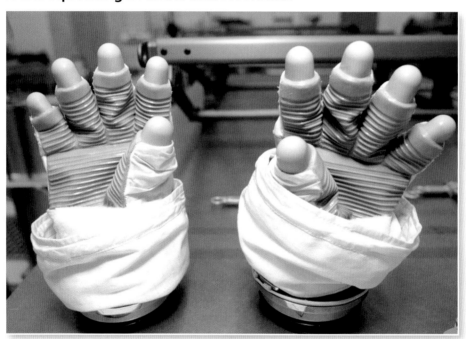

The first American space walk lasted only 23 minutes. It was made by Ed White on June 3, 1965.

Linda was glad she had eaten a good breakfast before her work began! Spacewalkers can be suited up for ten hours. During those long days, they get hungry. At one time, spacewalkers could bring snacks on their walks. The snacks were eraser-shaped and chewy. They made the inside of helmets messy, however, so they are no longer used.

"If you're lucky," says Linda, "your crewmates have fixed dinner for you [while you were spacewalking]."

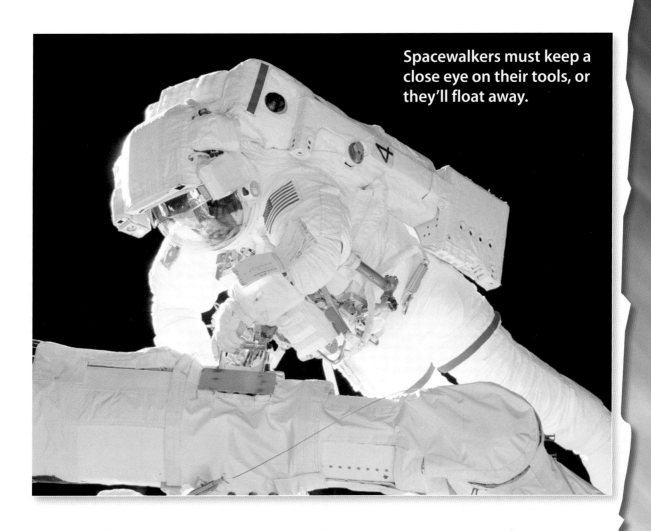

Spacewalkers must keep a close eye on their tools, or they'll float away.

Food Shortage on the ISS

Food is an important part of every astronaut's routine. The space shuttle used to carry food to the ISS on a regular basis. Then, in 2003, the shuttle *Columbia* broke apart during **reentry**. All on board were killed. NASA temporarily grounded the shuttle program. So, Russian **cargo** ships began to transport the food.

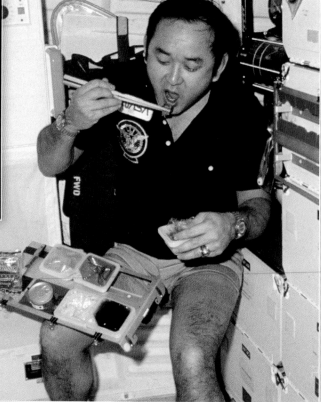

With his food tray strapped to his leg, an astronaut eats with chopsticks.

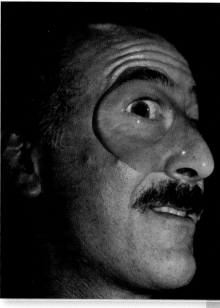

Astronaut Jeff Hoffman eyes a water blob.

In December 2004, food on the ISS ran short. A previous astronaut crew had eaten too much! Fortunately, for the new crew, a cargo ship soon delivered 400 pounds (181 kg) of things to eat. The delivery included turkey dinners for the holidays.

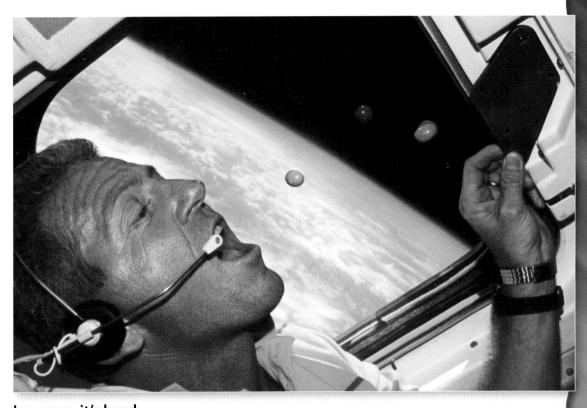

In space, it's hard to turn down the chance to play with food. Astronaut Loren Shriver enjoys floating candy.

The earlier ISS crew had permission to eat more when they found their diets boring. However, not all the extra food they ate was noted. So the later crew, at first, didn't realize there was a shortage.

"I See Downtown Houston!"

Worn-out but happy, Linda and Dan climbed down from the tower. They had spent 4 hours and 12 minutes in space. It was the final space walk of the year 2001. Looking down from the robot arm, they spotted a thrilling sight.

"I see downtown Houston!" called Dan. Houston, Texas, was home.

Endeavour landed back at the Kennedy Space Center on December 17, 2001.

The year 2001 holds the record for the greatest number of space walks— 12 from shuttles and 6 from the ISS.

Once they were back inside the spacecraft, the astronauts spoke with their families on Earth. Dan greeted his wife, and Linda said hello to her husband and daughter.

"Wow! What a fantastic day," said Dan. After six more days in space, the astronauts would blast home. Then they could greet their waiting families in person.

The STS-108 *Endeavour* crew
Front row: (*left*) Pilot Mark Kelly and Commander Dominic Gorie
Back row: (*left*) Spacewalkers Linda Godwin and Dan Tani

Just the Facts
MORE ABOUT SPACE EXPLORATION

- The world's first space walk almost ended in disaster. In 1965, Russian cosmonaut Alexi Leonov (ah-LEX-ee LEE-on-ove) became jammed in his spacecraft's airlock. He had to let out air from his space suit to squeeze through the hatch.

- It takes a spacewalker almost an hour to put on the space suit, and that's with help from another astronaut.

- No astronaut has ever been seriously hurt or killed while walking in space.

- At a distance of 240,000 miles (386,243 km), the moon is the farthest place that people have been from Earth. *Apollo* spacecraft made six separate missions to the moon between 1969 and 1972. In all, twelve astronauts walked on the surface of the moon.

Timeline

This timeline shows some important events in the young history of space walking.

1983
Story Musgrave tests the first space suit specially built for space walks.

1960   **1970**   **1980**

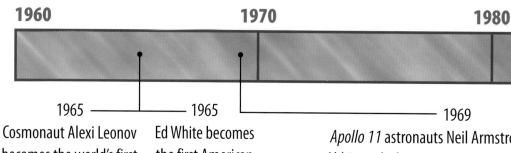

1965 — Cosmonaut Alexi Leonov becomes the world's first person to walk in space.

1965 — Ed White becomes the first American spacewalker.

1969 — *Apollo 11* astronauts Neil Armstrong and Buzz Aldrin make historic space walks on the surface of the moon. Their footprints are still there!

- American Shannon Lucid holds the record for the most days in space by a woman. She spent 188 days on the space station *Mir*.

- The STS-108 *Endeavour* mission was Dan Tani's first time in space.

- Aboard the STS-108 *Endeavour* was an American flag. It had been found in the World Trade Center ruins after the terrorist attack on September 11, 2001.

Ed White, the first American spacewalker

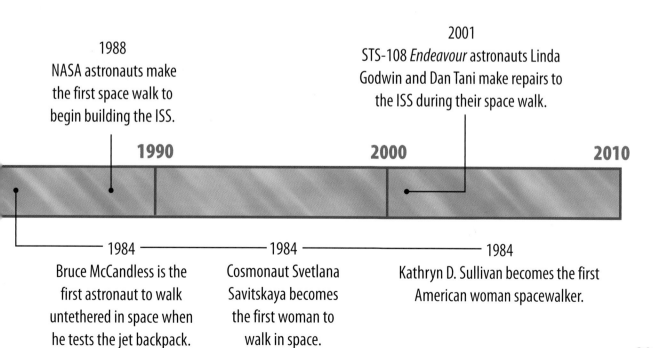

1988
NASA astronauts make the first space walk to begin building the ISS.

2001
STS-108 *Endeavour* astronauts Linda Godwin and Dan Tani make repairs to the ISS during their space walk.

1990

2000

2010

1984
Bruce McCandless is the first astronaut to walk untethered in space when he tests the jet backpack.

1984
Cosmonaut Svetlana Savitskaya becomes the first woman to walk in space.

1984
Kathryn D. Sullivan becomes the first American woman spacewalker.

GLOSSARY

airlock (AIR-lok) an airtight area with two doors, one to the shuttle and one to the outside, that allows astronauts to change air-pressure levels

cargo (KAR-goh) a load of goods or supplies

equator (i-KWAY-tur) the imaginary line around the middle of Earth

gravity (GRAV-uh-tee) the force that pulls things toward Earth, the sun, or other bodies in space

International Space Station (*in*-tur-NASH-uh-nuhl SPAYSS STAY-shun) a research base in space, where astronauts from different countries live and work

NASA (NA-suh) the National Aeronautics and Space Administration, the organization responsible for U.S. activities in space

orbits (OR-bits) the path of an object that is circling a planet or the sun

pressurized (PRESH-ur-rized) made to keep air in a sealed environment such as a space suit

reentry (ree-EN-tree) returning to Earth's atmosphere

robot arm (ROH-bot ARM) a mechanical arm attached to a space shuttle or space station

solar system (SOH-lur SISS-tuhm) the sun and everything that circles around it in orbit, including the nine planets

solar wings (SOH-lur WINGZ) huge panels made up of cells that use the sun's energy to provide power

space shuttle (SPAYSS SHUHT-uhl) a reusable spacecraft that carries people, supplies, and equipment into space

tethered (TETH-urd) tied or attached by a line; in space, the safety line keeps astronauts from floating away

thermal (THUR-muhl) made to hold in heat

vastness (VAST-ness) huge size, area, or amount

weightless (WATE-liss) having very little or no weight, especially because of little or no gravity

BIBLIOGRAPHY

Caprara, Giovanni. *Living in Space: From Science Fiction to the International Space Station.* Buffalo, NY: Firefly Books (2000).

Chaikin, Andrew. *Space: A History of Space Exploration in Photographs.* Buffalo, NY: Firefly Books (2004).

Glover, Linda K. *National Geographic Encyclopedia of Space.* Washington, D.C.: National Geographic (2004).

Halvorson, Todd. *"Endeavour Spacewalkers Step Through Station Repair Work."* December 10, 2001. **www.space.com/missionlaunches/sts108_pm_011210.html**

Reichhardt, Tony, ed. *Space Shuttle: The First 20 Years—The Astronauts' Experiences in Their Own Words.* New York: DK Publishing (2002).

Woodmansee, Laura S. *Women Astronauts* (book and CD of movies and interviews). Burlington, Ontario, Canada: Collector's Guide Publishing (2002).

READ MORE

Bond, Peter. *DK Guide to Space.* New York: DK Publishing (1999).

Maze, Stephanie. *I Want to Be an Astronaut.* New York: Harcourt (1997).

Schyffert, Bea Uusma. *The Man Who Went to the Far Side of the Moon: The Story of Apollo 11 Astronaut Michael Collins.* San Francisco, CA: Chronicle Books (2003).

Simon, Seymour. *The Universe.* New York: HarperTrophy (2000).

Spangenburg, Ray, and Kit Moser. *Onboard the Space Shuttle.* New York: Franklin Watts (2002).

Yes Magazine, **eds.** *The Amazing International Space Station.* Toronto, Ontario, Canada: Kids Can Press (2003).

LEARN MORE ONLINE

Visit these Web sites to learn more about surviving in space:

science.howstuffworks.com/space-suit5.htm

www1.edspace.nasa.gov/text/astroschool/survival/

www.pbs.org/spacestation/

www.spaceflight.nasa.gov/home/index.html

INDEX

ABOUT THE AUTHOR

A former school librarian, Donna Latham is a writer in the Chicago, Illinois, area. One of her favorite childhood memories is of watching the *Apollo 11* moon landing on TV.

Quilt Notes

DESIGNS BY PEARL LOUISE KRUSH

If you can sew and if you love fabric and quilts, you'll enjoy making soft, warm rugs for your home. Pearl Louise Krush has designed seven rugs for this book that vary from patchwork-pieced quilted rugs to woven and rag rugs. All are easily made, even by beginners, but some may take more time than others.

Take a look around your house. Where might a dash of color or a welcoming threshold benefit from a new rug? Dig into your stash for a traditional raggy look, or incorporate upholstery or drapery fabrics for a designer look. You'll love the results!

CAUTION: Place rug in low-traffic area of your home or spray with rug backing to eliminate the possibility of slipping.

General Instructions

Fabric Selection
All of the rugs in this book are made of 100 percent cotton fabrics. You may certainly decide to use other fabrics, but be sure the fabric you use is colorfast and has some substance. Lightweight fabrics won't hold their shape after laundering, and they are also difficult to work with when constructing the rug. Heavier-weight cottons, like homespuns and flannels, work especially well.

All materials are based on 44"-wide fabric.

Batting
If batting is required, a good choice is Warm & Natural cotton batting. Two or three layers of this batting give the rug a good weight and make it soft to step on. The quilting is more defined when you use at least two layers of batting.

Thread
Use cotton or poly-cotton blend all-purpose thread to sew the components of each rug together. A strong quilting thread or buttonhole thread is recommended for all handwork.

Tools
Rotary-cutting tools (rotary cutter, cutting mat and quilter's acrylic gridded ruler) are necessary for making rugs. You will also need sharp scissors and basic sewing supplies.

Seams
Use ¼" seams throughout unless otherwise instructed.

Pressing
Press all seams toward the darker fabric when possible.

Quilting
A walking foot for your sewing machine and a heavier machine needle are highly recommended when sewing with the thickness of fabrics and batting required for each rug. ■

Rose Garden Rug

The blending of soft plaids and florals in this rug would make it especially nice for a bedroom or bathroom. Add a nonskid pad on slick surfaces.

Project Specifications
Skill Level: Beginner
Rug Size: 42" x 36"

Fabric & Batting
- 1 fat quarter each rose, yellow and green prints for appliqué
- ½ yard melon homespun plaid
- 1 yard cream solid
- 1¾ yards light green homespun plaid
- 2 thin batting rectangles 46" x 40"

Supplies & Tools
- Rotary-cutting tools
- 1 yard fusible web
- 5 yards 3"-wide cream fringe
- All-purpose thread to blend with fabrics
- Machine-embroidery thread to match appliqué fabrics
- Natural quilting thread
- Basic sewing supplies

Instructions
1. From light green homespun plaid, cut one backing rectangle 46" x 40". Put aside.

2. From light green and melon homespun plaids, cut 10 squares each 7¼" x 7¼". Draw a diagonal line across the wrong side of the melon squares.

3. Place each melon square on a green plaid square, right sides facing. Sew a ¼" seam each side of drawn line. Cut on line, open and press.

4. Draw a diagonal line across the wrong side of ten of the half-square triangles, perpendicular to the seam line. Pair the squares, right sides facing, with a melon triangle facing a green triangle. Sew a ¼" seam each side of drawn line. Cut on line, open and press to make 20 quarter-square triangles.

5. Referring to Placement Diagram, arrange four rows of five squares each. Sew squares together in each row and then join rows.

6. From cream solid, cut two strips each 6½" x 24½" and 6½" x 42½" for borders.

7. Trace appliqué shapes on paper side of fusible web as instructed on pattern. Cut out, leaving roughly ¼" margin around traced shapes.

8. Fuse shapes on selected fabrics as instructed by manufacturer. Cut out on traced lines. Referring to Placement Diagram, arrange appliqué pieces on borders and fuse.

9. Machine-embroider around appliqué shapes with matching thread.

10. Sew short borders to opposite sides of rug. Sew long borders to top and bottom; press.

11. Layer backing, two layers of batting and rug top. Quilt as desired.

12. Trim batting even with top of rug. Trim excess

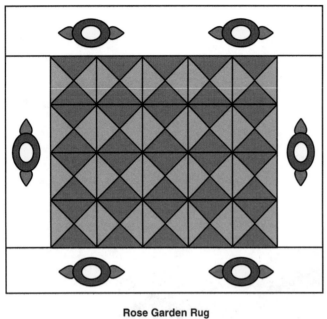

Rose Garden Rug
Placement Diagram
42" x 36"

backing fabric leaving 1" of fabric around all edges. Fold back ¼"; press. Fold again and stitch to the top of the rug.

13. Sew fringe to perimeter of rug. ■

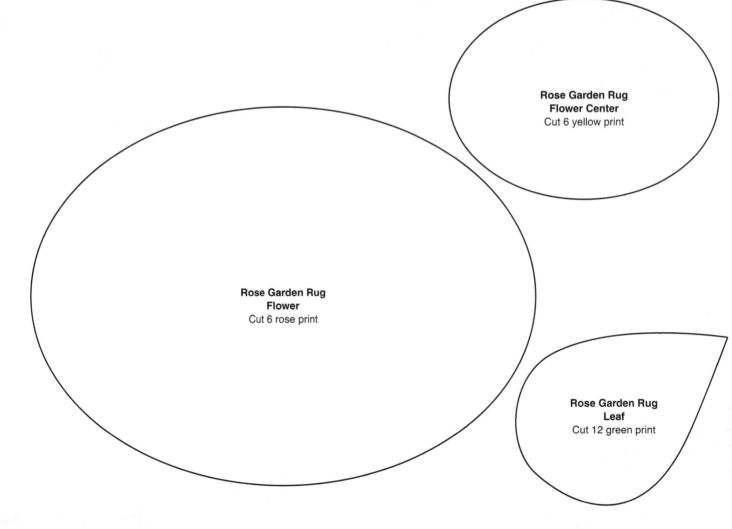

Rose Garden Rug
Flower Center
Cut 6 yellow print

Rose Garden Rug
Flower
Cut 6 rose print

Rose Garden Rug
Leaf
Cut 12 green print

Welcome Home Rug

This rug will look great at any entrance of your home. It's an open invitation for not only visitors, but your family as well.

Project Specifications
Skill Level: Beginner
Rug Size: 34" x 24"

Fabric & Batting
- Fat quarter rust print for letters
- 1 fat quarter each of 4 different brown prints
- ¼ yard tan checked background print
- ¼ yard cream-and-red print for Welcome borders and cornerstones
- 1¼ yards brown print for border and backing
- 2 thin batting rectangles 38½" x 28"

Welcome Home Rug
Placement Diagram
34" x 24"

Supplies & Tools
- Rotary-cutting tools
- 1 yard fusible web
- All-purpose thread to blend with fabrics
- Machine-embroidery thread to match appliqué letters
- Brown quilting thread
- Basic sewing supplies

Instructions
1. Trace letters on paper side of fusible web. Cut out, leaving roughly ¼" margin around traced lines. Fuse to rust print following manufacturer's instructions. Cut out on traced lines.

2. From tan checked background print, cut one rectangle 6½" x 30½". Referring to Placement Diagram, arrange letters on background rectangle. Allow at least ½" on all sides for seam allowance. When satisfied with arrangement, fuse in place.

3. Sew a satin stitch, narrow zigzag or other decorative stitch around letters.

4. From cream-and-red print, cut two border strips 1½" x 30½". Sew to top and bottom of appliqué panel.

5. From one brown print fat quarter, cut four squares 6½" x 6½". From three remaining brown print fat quarters, cut two squares each 6½" x 6½".

6. Referring to the Placement Diagram, sew two strips of five squares each, matching fabrics on each end of both strips; press.

7. Sew one strip to top and bottom of Welcome strip.

8. From brown border print, cut two strips each 2½" x 20½" and 2½" x 30½". Sew longer strips to top and bottom of rug. From cream-and-red print,

cut four squares 2½" x 2½". Sew one square to each end of remaining border strips. Sew to short sides of rug.

9. From brown border print, cut one backing rectangle 38½" x 28". Layer batting rectangles between backing and pieced top. Baste and quilt as desired.

10. Trim batting even with rug top. Trim backing, leaving 1" allowance around all edges.

11. Fold outer edge of backing allowance under ¼" and press. Fold again to the top edge of the rug and sew in place. ■

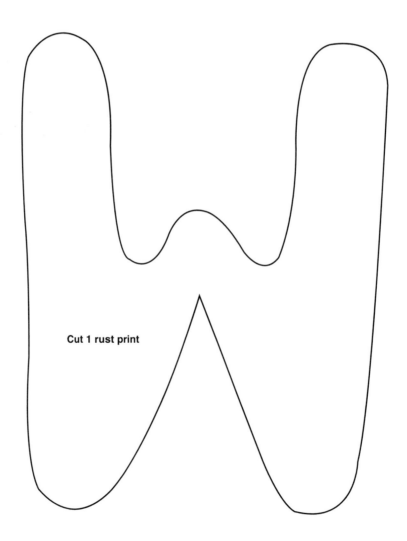

Cut 1 rust print

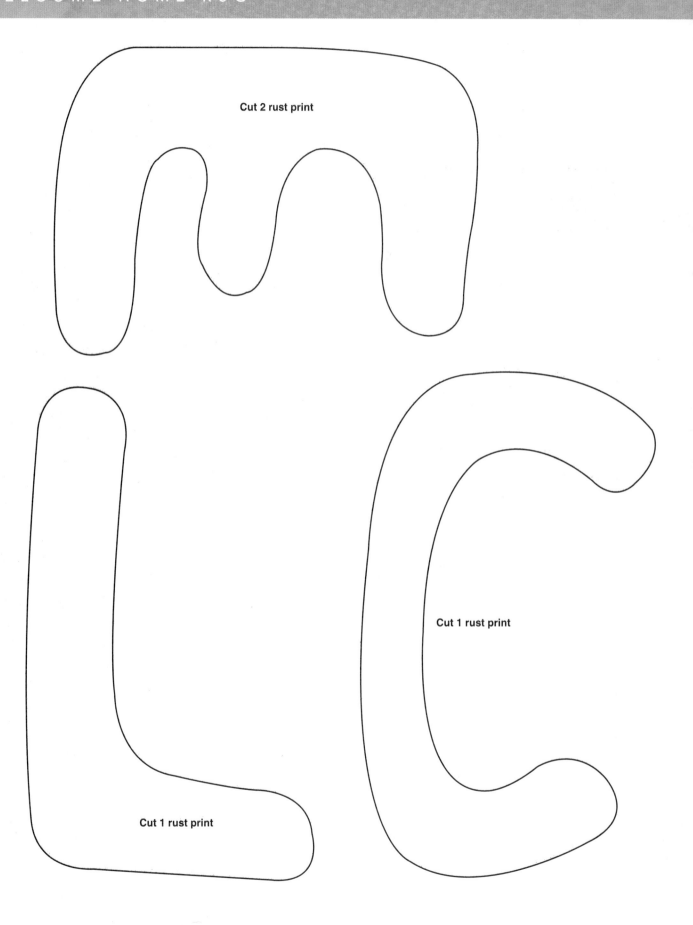

Cut 2 rust print

Cut 1 rust print

Cut 1 rust print

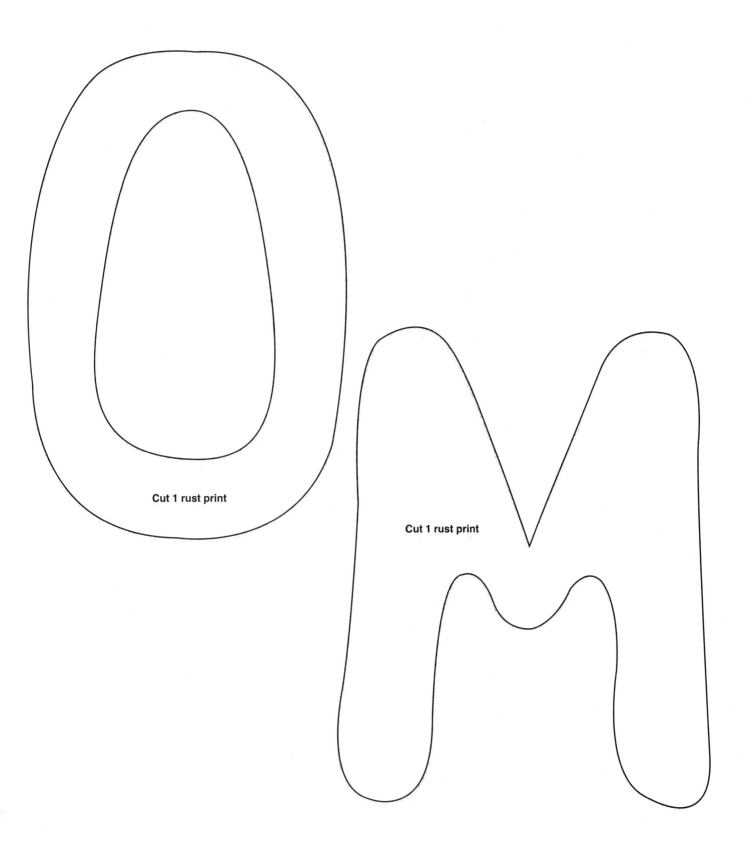

Cut 1 rust print

Cut 1 rust print

Oval Shag Rug

This rug is all about texture! It's lovely in cream, but just imagine the color possibilities.

Project Specifications
Skill Level: Beginner
Rug Size: 30" x 24"

Fabric & Batting
- 6 yards cream solid heavyweight cotton
- 2 thin batting rectangles 36" x 26"

Supplies & Tools
- Rotary-cutting tools
- 2½ yards ½"-wide cream braid
- All-purpose thread to blend with fabrics
- Basic sewing supplies

Instructions
1. From cream solid, cut two rectangles 36" x 26". Fold each rectangle in quarters and use pattern to cut two ovals. Use pattern again to cut two ovals from batting rectangles.

2. Place batting ovals between fabric layers. Pin to secure.

3. From cream solid fabric, cut enough 3"-wide bias strips and join to make 2½ yards of binding. Fold lengthwise, wrong sides facing; press. Align raw edges and sew binding around outer edge of rug on right side. Bring fold to back of rug and machine-stitch in place. Remove pins.

4. From cream solid fabric, cut 1500 squares 2" x 2". Fold each in half to form triangles.

5. In a line across the center of the top of the rug, place the folded edge of each triangle on top of the pointed end of the next triangle, overlapping about ½". Sew 24 folded squares into a straight line as shown in Figure 1.

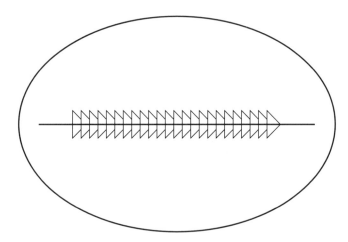

Figure 1
Sew 24 folded squares, overlapped, in a straight line down the center of the oval.

6. Continue overlapping and sewing folded squares in rows about ½" apart, spiraling in an oval around the centerline and working toward the outside of the oval. The final row of squares will flair out with the points extending beyond the fabric oval.

7. Sew ½"-wide braid over the final sewn line on the outer edge of the rug. ■

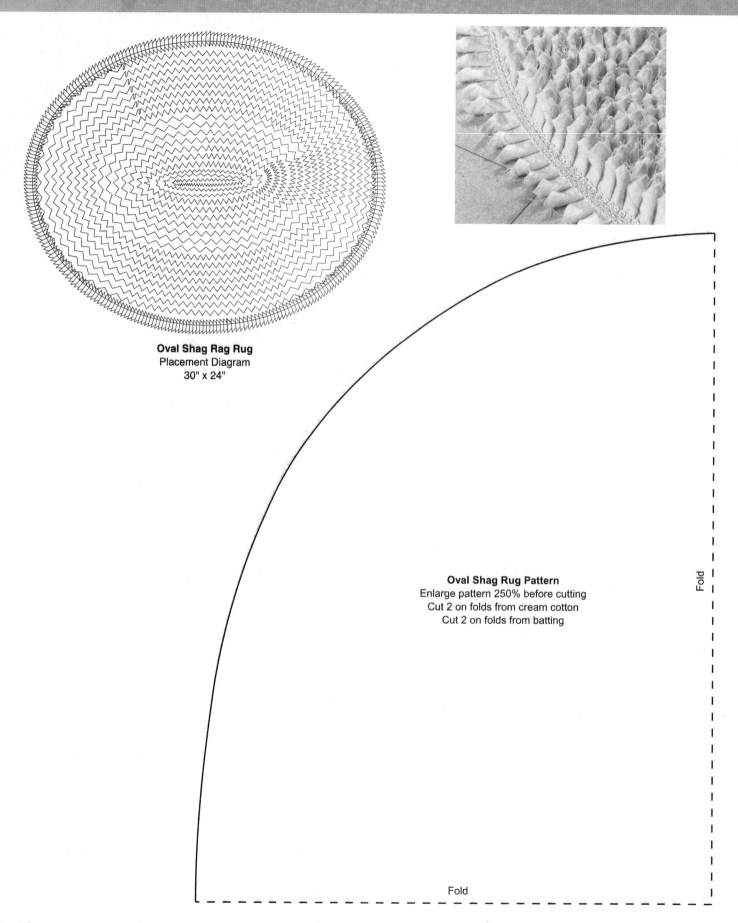

Oval Shag Rag Rug
Placement Diagram
30" x 24"

Oval Shag Rug Pattern
Enlarge pattern 250% before cutting
Cut 2 on folds from cream cotton
Cut 2 on folds from batting

Fold

Fold

HOUSE OF WHITE BIRCHES, BERNE, INDIANA 46711　WWW.WHITEBIRCHES.COM

Bear Paw Raggy Rug

The chenille technique used in this North Woods-style rug makes it ever so soft to step on.

Project Specifications
Skill Level: Beginner
Rug Size: Approximately 30" x 38"

Fabric & Batting
- Rust print fat quarter for Bear Paw corners
- ⅓ yard green print flannel for Bear Paw corners
- ⅔ yard each of five different homespun plaids for chenille center
- 1 yard North Woods print flannel for borders
- 2 yards thin cotton batting

Supplies & Tools
- Rotary-cutting tools
- Sharp scissors
- All-purpose thread to blend with fabrics
- Quilting thread to blend with fabrics
- Basic sewing supplies

Instructions
1. From each of the five different homespun plaids, cut one rectangle 19" x 27". From thin cotton batting, cut two rectangles 18" x 26".

2. Place one of the homespun plaids face down on work surface. This piece will be the backing.

3. Place two batting rectangles on top of backing.

4. Layer four remaining homespun rectangles right side up on top of batting.

5. By machine, quilt all layers together by sewing diagonal seams ½" apart over entire piece, alternating direction of quilting as shown in Figure 1. You may be able to use a plaid line as a guide.

6. Carefully insert the sharp scissors blade between the third and fourth fabric layers. Cut through the top three layers of fabric between stitching lines.

Bear Paw Raggy Rug
Placement Diagram
Approximately 30" x 38"

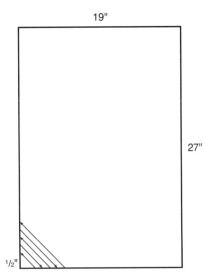

Figure 1
Quilt layers diagonally, alternating
direction of quilting as shown.

7. From green print flannel, cut four
squares 4¾" x 4¾", four squares 2⅞" x
2⅞" and eight squares 2½" x 2½". From
the rust print fat quarter, cut four squares
2⅞" x 2⅞", four squares 2½" x 2½" and
eight rectangles 2½" x 2¾".

8. Draw a diagonal line across the back of
the 2⅞" green print squares. Place right
sides together with 2⅞" rust print squares.
Sew ¼" seam on each side of drawn line.
Cut on line and press to make eight half-
square triangles.

9. To make the A squares of each block,
draw a diagonal line across the back of a 2½"
green print square. Align at right-hand side of a
2½" x 2¾" rust print rectangle. Sew from bottom
left to top right on drawn line. Trim seam to ¼".
Open and press. Repeat for four units.

10. To make the B squares of each block, draw a
diagonal line across the back of a 2½" green print
square. Align with the left-hand side of a 2½" x

2¾" rust print rectangle. Sew on the line from
lower right to upper left. Trim seam to ¼". Open
and press. Repeat for four units.

11. Arrange all squares as shown in Figure 2 and
sew together. Note that two seam allowances are
½" to allow for frayed seams.

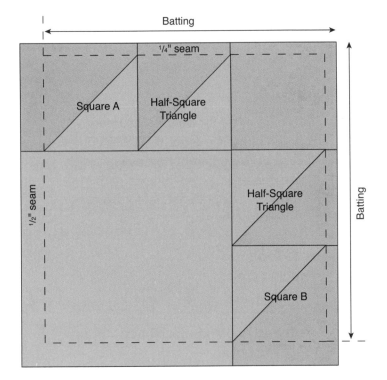

Figure 2
Arrange squares as shown, noting
seam allowances.

▶ Continued on page 23

Woven Wonders Rug

In addition to being very attractive, this unique and very distinctive rug will hold up well to heavy traffic.

Project Specifications
Skill Level: Beginner
Rug Size: 43½" x 21½"

Fabric & Batting
- 1½ yards dark tan homespun
- 2 yards dark blue plaid homespun
- 3 yards thin cotton batting

Supplies & Tools
- Rotary-cutting tools
- All-purpose thread to blend with fabrics
- Dark tan quilting thread
- Basic sewing supplies

Instructions

1. From dark blue plaid homespun, cut 11 strips 4½" x 44". From dark tan homespun, cut 20 strips 4½" x 22".

2. From batting, cut 40 strips 2" x 22" and 22 strips 2" x 44".

3. Place the 4½" x 44" fabric strips right side down on work surface. Place two 2" strips of batting down the center of each strip of fabric.

4. Fold the fabric to the center. Overlap and fold under the top fabric ¼" Sew down the center of the strip to hold all fabric and batting layers together. Repeat for all fabric strips.

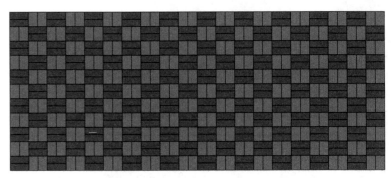

Woven Wonders Rug
Placement Diagram
43½" x 21½"

5. Place 11 dark blue plaid homespun strips side by side on work surface. Starting at one end of the dark blue plaid homespun strips, weave a dark tan strip over and under the blue strips and pin in place. Continue weaving as tightly as possible until all strips are used.

6. Pin the ends of each strip in place all around the outer edge of the rug.

7. From dark blue plaid homespun, cut four 3"-wide strips across the width of the fabric. Join end to end for binding strip. Fold in half lengthwise; press. Align the raw edges of the binding with the raw edges of the rug on the right side and sew, mitering the corners.

8. Bring folded edge of binding to back of rug and machine-sew in place. ■

Circling Geese Denim Rug

The flying geese are traditional, the stripes are nautical and denim is everyone's favorite. This rug will be a hit in any home.

Project Specifications
Skill Level: Beginner
Rug Size: 27" x 36"

Fabric & Batting
- ½ yard blue paisley print
- ½ yard red paisley print
- ⅔ yard red-and-blue striped ticking
- 1½ yards blue embossed denim
- 2 thin batting rectangles 32" x 42"

Supplies & Tools
- Rotary-cutting tools
- All-purpose thread to blend with fabrics
- Natural quilting thread
- Basic sewing supplies

Instructions

1. From blue embossed denim, cut one rug backing rectangle 32" x 42" and put aside. Cut 54 squares 3½" x 3½". From red and blue paisley prints, cut 13 rectangles each 3½" x 6½". Draw a diagonal line across the backside of each square.

2. Place a blue embossed denim square cut in step 1 on the right-hand side of one of the paisley rectangles, right sides facing. Sew on the drawn line as shown in Figure 1. Open and press. Trim, leaving a ¼" seam allowance.

3. Place a second blue embossed denim square on the left side of the rectangle and stitch as shown in Figure 2. Open and press. Trim, leaving a ¼" seam allowance. Repeat for 13 Flying Geese units of each color as shown in Figure 3.

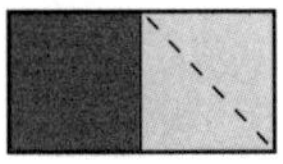

Figure 1
Sew on line as shown.

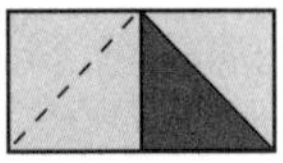

Figure 2
Sew on line as shown.

Make 13   Make 13

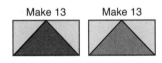

Figure 3
Make 26 Flying Geese units as shown.

4. From embossed blue denim, cut 10 squares 6½" x 6½". From red-and-blue striped ticking, cut seven rectangles 3½" x 6½".

5. Referring to Placement Diagram, arrange all pieces as shown. Sew Flying Geese units together in strips. Sew rows together and then join rows.

6. Layer batting rectangles between backing and pieced top. Baste and quilt as desired. Trim

▶ Continued on page 23

Ohio Star Welcome Rug

The large-sized pieces in this rug make construction a snap! Vary the fabrics and colors to fit the theme of any room.

Project Specifications
Skill Level: Beginner
Rug Size: 36" x 36"

Fabric & Batting
- ½ yard brown plaid
- ½ yard dark green check for star points
- 1 yard dark tan print
- 1¾ yards red plaid for border and backing
- 2 squares thin cotton batting 40" x 40"

Supplies & Tools
- Rotary-cutting tools
- All-purpose thread to blend with fabrics
- Dark green quilting thread
- Basic sewing supplies

Instructions
1. From brown plaid and dark green check, cut eight squares each 6½" x 6½". Draw a diagonal line across the backside of each square.

2. From dark tan print, cut four rectangles 6½" x 12½". Place a dark green square cut in step 1 on the right-hand side of one of the rectangles, right sides facing. Sew on the drawn line as shown in Figure 1. Open and press. Trim, leaving a ¼" seam allowance.

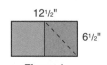

Figure 1
Sew on line as shown.

3. Place a second dark green square on the left side of the rectangle and stitch as shown in Figure 2. Open and press. Trim, leaving a ¼" seam allowance. Repeat for four star-point units as shown in Figure 3.

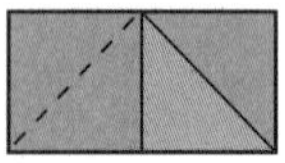

Figure 2
Sew on line as shown.

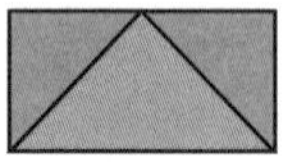

Figure 3
Make 4 star points as shown.

4. From dark tan print, cut one center square 12½" x 12½". Sew one star-point unit to two opposite sides of center square.

5. From dark tan print, cut eight squares 6½" x 6½". Sew one to each end of two star-point units to make a strip as shown in Figure 4. Sew to top and bottom of center square.

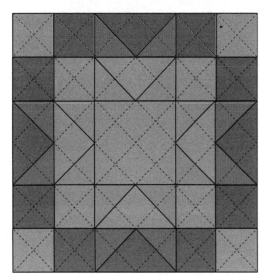

Ohio Star Welcome Rug
Placement Diagram
36" x 36"

Figure 4
Make strip as shown.

6. From red plaid, cut one square 40" x 40"

and put aside for backing; cut four 6½" x 12½" rectangles and eight 6½" x 6½" squares.

7. Sew the brown plaid squares cut in step 1 to the red plaid rectangles by the same method as in steps 2 and 3 above, making secondary star-point units.

8. Sew a 6½" red plaid square to the ends of each secondary star-point unit for borders. Sew two borders to opposite sides of rug. Sew a dark tan print square to the ends of two remaining borders and sew to top and bottom of rug.

9. Layer two 40" batting squares between pieced top and backing. Pin or baste and quilt as desired.

10. Trim batting even with rug top. Trim backing, leaving 1" allowance around all edges.

11. Fold outer edge of backing allowance under ¼" and press. Fold again to the top edge of the rug and sew in place. ∎

Bear Paw Raggy Rug
Continued from page 14

12. From North Woods print, cut four rectangles each 6¾" x 19" and 6¾" x 27". Cut four squares 6¾" x 6¾". From thin cotton batting, cut four rectangles each 6¼" x 18" and 6¼" x 26".

13. Layer two batting pieces between two fabric rectangles of the same size. Quilt as desired to within ½" of edges.

14. Layer two batting squares between a North Woods square and a Bear Paw square. Refer to Figure 2 and remember to allow ½" seam allowances on two sides of the block. Quilt as desired to within ½" on two sides and ¼" on the remaining two sides. Repeat for four corner squares.

15. Sew a Bear Paw square to each short border using ½" seam allowance and with the seams up.

16. Sew the long borders to the chenille center panel with the seams up.

17. Sew the top and bottom borders to the rug with ½" seam allowance and the seams up.

18. From green print flannel, cut four 2½"-wide strips across the width of the fabric. Sew end to end for binding strip.

19. Fold binding strip lengthwise, wrong sides facing; press. Sew the raw edges to the front outer edge of the rug, mitering at the corners.

20. Turn the folded edge of the binding to the back of the rug and sew in place by hand or machine. ◼

Circling Geese Denim Rug
Continued from page 18

all edges even with the pieced top.

7. From red-and-blue striped ticking, cut four 2½"-wide strips across the width of the fabric. Sew them together end to end for one long binding strip.

8. Fold binding strip lengthwise, wrong sides facing; press. Sew the raw edges to the front outer edge of the rug, mitering at the corners.

9. Turn the folded edge of the binding to the back of the rug and sew in place by hand or machine. ◼

Circling Geese Denim Rug
Placement Diagram
27" x 36"

Meet the Designer

Pearl Louise Krush

Pearl Louise Krush has been involved with the craft and quilting industries for over 17 years. She began her involvement by joining the Society of Craft Designers in 1985. That same year, Pearl started her own pattern company and named it Pearl Louise Designs. She also began participating in the International Quilt Market. Five years ago, she opened Thimble Cottage Quilt Shop. It is located in the Black Hills of South Dakota, which is about 25 miles from Mount Rushmore.

Even though Pearl is an entrepreneur, she still manages to find time for many other projects. She has designed items for *Craft World*, and has worked as a project designer for Queen Craft Lace and Wyla Lace. She continues to design for craft and quilt product companies nationwide. Pearl also enjoys organizing many quilting events. She loves inspiring others to create and to share various techniques of hand and machine sewing, and quilting.

When Pearl isn't quilting, designing or running her companies, she enjoys spending time outdoors. Gardening and fishing with her husband, Fred, are just a couple of her favorite pastimes. She lives in Rapid City, S.D., where she and her husband enjoy spending time with their three sons, daughters-in-law and wonderful grandchildren.

E-mail: Customer_Service@whitebirches.com

Step-On-It Rugs is published by House of White Birches, 306 East Parr Road, Berne, IN 46711, telephone (260) 589-4000. Printed in USA. Copyright © 2003 House of White Birches.

RETAILERS: If you would like to carry this pattern book or any other House of White Birches publications, call the Wholesale Department at Annie's Attic to set up a direct account: (903) 636-4303. Also, request a complete listing of publications available from House of White Birches.

Every effort has been made to ensure that the instructions in this pattern book are complete and accurate. We cannot, however, take responsibility for human error, typographical mistakes or variations in individual work.

ISBN: 1-59217-028-5
1 2 3 4 5 6 7 8 9

STAFF
Editor: Jeanne Stauffer
Associate Editor: Dianne Schmidt
Technical Editor: Mary Jo Kurten
Technical Artist: Chad Summers
Copy Editors: Michelle Beck, Nicki Lehman
Graphic Arts Supervisor: Ronda Bechinski
Graphic Artist: Erin Augsburger
Photography: Tammy Christian, Kelly Heydinger, Christena Green
Photo Stylist: Tammy Nussbaum

Metric Conversion Charts

Metric Conversions

U.S. Measurements		Multiplied by		Metric Measurement
yards	x	.9144	=	meters (m)
yards	x	91.44	=	centimeters (cm)
inches	x	2.54	=	centimeters (cm)
inches	x	25.40	=	millimeters (mm)
inches	x	.0254	=	meters (m)

Metric Measurements		Multiplied by		U.S. Measurements
centimeters	x	.3937	=	inches
meters	x	1.0936	=	yards

Standard Equivalents

U.S. Measurement		Metric Measurement		
1/8 inch	=	3.20 mm	=	0.32 cm
1/4 inch	=	6.35 mm	=	0.635 cm
3/8 inch	=	9.50 mm	=	0.95 cm
1/2 inch	=	12.70 mm	=	1.27 cm
5/8 inch	=	15.90 mm	=	1.59 cm
3/4 inch	=	19.10 mm	=	1.91 cm
7/8 inch	=	22.20 mm	=	2.22 cm
1 inch	=	25.40 mm	=	2.54 cm
1/8 yard	=	11.43 cm	=	0.11 m
1/4 yard	=	22.86 cm	=	0.23 m
3/8 yard	=	34.29 cm	=	0.34 m
1/2 yard	=	45.72 cm	=	0.46 m
5/8 yard	=	57.15 cm	=	0.57 m
3/4 yard	=	68.58 cm	=	0.69 m
7/8 yard	=	80.00 cm	=	0.80 m
1 yard	=	91.44 cm	=	0.91 m